FEED YOUR
SPIRIT

KATHERINE SCHNEIDER

Copyright © 2022 by Feed Your Spirit LTD

All rights reserved.

ISBN: 979-8-9873904-0-5

For my mother, Pamela

I love you

CONTENTS

-	Remember who you are	Pg 7
-	Introduction	Pg 9
1	January	Pg 11
2	February	Pg 29
3	March	Pg 47
4	April	Pg 65
5	May	Pg 81
6	June	Pg 95
7	July	Pg 109
8	August	Pg 125
9	September	Pg 139
10	October	Pg 153
11	November	Pg 169
12	December	Pg 183
-	Resources	Pg 197

REMEMBER WHO YOU ARE

You were born without a care in the world.
Full of mystery and potential, your story was untold.

As you grew up, there were no limits to who you could be.
A firefighter, a fairy, your ending was yet to see.

You laughed, you played, the world was your stage.
Little did you know life would be very different as you aged.

As your years went on, you were told what to do.
Programmed by the media, family, and a well-meaning few.

The adults around you seemed to have it all wrong.
But you ignored your own guidance, too many were gone.

Your resistance was called the teenage years.
This was your last chance to live free, free without fears.

Now you are grown, and life isn't much fun.
You used to laugh and play when now there is none.

Your mind is clouded by negative fears.
The many thoughts and feelings passed on by your peers.

You know something is wrong. You know there is more.
But positive thinking doesn't offer any cure.

Now that your mind is trained into submission.
These years of programming will need a hard revision.

- Feed Your Spirit

FEED YOUR SPIRIT

INTRODUCTION

Changing the way you think and breaking habits of thought takes practice, just like learning to ride a bike or speak a new language.

This book of daily inspirations takes you on a journey to learn the language of self-love, happiness, inner peace, and balance one day at a time.

Your year of inspiration starts now!

It doesn't matter on which day and month you begin. Whenever you have chosen to pick up this book and start your journey is the right time for **you**.

Read your inspiration daily, preferably in the morning when first waking up, as this is the best way to start your day with positive intentions.

If you happen to miss a day, know that you didn't need to hear the message for that day and continue the next day. There is no need to go back in time to read and try to process yesterday's message. The inspiration you need will arrive on the correct day for you.

While it is best to focus on one message a day, if you need extra guidance or the answer to a question, intend to find the message you need to hear, then skim the pages landing on a random inspiration. If you have clearly intended to hear what is right for you now, **trust** the message you receive.

You may find some inspirations you will hear and others you may resist. Pay attention to the messages you resist, as this may be showing you areas of struggle and can be an opportunity for growth. Ask yourself, what do I need to learn from this message? Where am I blocked?

Starting on this journey takes just a few minutes a day. Imagine how much your life can change when you free your mind from limiting beliefs that are holding you back and start remembering just how **powerful** you really are.

The life you are dreaming about is here. The happiness is here. The fun is here. The success is here, and the balance is here. It's time to connect, let go, and allow all the good to flow into your life!

To help you along the way, we have created a powerful set of 15-minute meditations specifically designed to reprogram your mindset, helping to remove and replace unconscious beliefs that may be holding you back. If you choose to include meditation with your daily inspirations, you can visit **feedyourspirit.com/meditation** for a free weekly meditation to help you get started.

Let's begin!

JANUARY

The new year brings in an energy of freshness. Would you like to have a fresh start? A new beginning? A New You?

As a child, you believed you could be anything you wanted to be, but somewhere along the way, as you heard the voices of others and society, you lost that faith – that **belief** in yourself.

Can you remember when you lost hope?

This new year brings with it a fresh start, so start imagining beyond your wildest dreams! What would you like to be different? Visualize it. See it as really happening. Imagine your life one year from now, living it exactly as you want it to be.

With a little shift in your thinking, you can transform your life. The power is in your hands. The time is now. Let's go!

FEED YOUR SPIRIT

January 1

You possess more power than you realize.

Your possibilities are far greater than you think.

When you visualize, you open the door to all that you want.

So, who do you want to be?

January 2

Your life is in a rapid state of transformation. The energy of the universe is sending you everything you want.

This may feel uncomfortable for a minute.

You may even feel some fear or worry arise.

This is your reminder to **trust** what is happening and let in all you have been asking for. You have asked, and it is being given.

This is just the start... Can you feel it?

January 3

Take a moment of stillness today and allow yourself to rest in silence without the mental noise of your thoughts.

As you are still, become aware of this space, and feel it fully.

If any thoughts pop into your mind, let them go and become still again.

In this space, you are connected to your source.

What is it telling you?

January 4

Love is the most powerful vibrational frequency.

When you send love out to others, your relationships will improve.

When you send love to your bills, you will attract more money to pay them.

And, when you love yourself, you will attract others who love you too.

January 5

You cannot change another person, but you can change the **version** of them that shows up for you.

Everybody has a calm, friendly, loving side, and everybody can get angry or annoyed. The side of others showing up for you is a good indication of where you are.

If you are in a bad mood, you will likely catch others who are in a bad mood. You are in sync with their energy.

The same goes for when you are feeling good, your energy is in-sync with others that feel good, and that's whom you are more likely to interact with.

If you are around negative people, you are a match to that side of them. When you blame the other person, you are not fixing what is happening.

Instead, try to uplift your energy in any way that works for you. Meditate, use positive affirmations, and think nice thoughts about others around you as you go about your day.

Doing this will not only **attract** better people into your life, but it will also impact the people who are already in your life, they will feel your positive energy, and they will shift too!

January 6

When you feel grateful for all you have, you open the door for more to come to you.

The universe **loves** grateful energy.

Gratitude helps to improve your self-esteem and your psychological health and opens the door to more fulfilling relationships in your life.

Think of all you have to be grateful for today.

January 7

Trust your instincts, and you will never need to worry about making a mistake. Your instincts are guiding you along the way.

Don't be afraid to say no.

Don't be afraid to say yes.

You've got this!

January 8

Miracles happen every day.

As a child, you expected miracles, and you believed in the **magic** of life.

Never stop believing.

January 9

You can spend your time around "positive people" because you want to keep your vibration high, or you can raise yourself up so much that you will naturally be uplifting to all around you.

Then instead of an us versus them mentality, you will **naturally** bring people into a new way of seeing the world, and this is a beautiful thing.

January 10

Open your heart and learn to trust again.

Even if you have been let down in the past.

The past is over. Decide to let it go today.

January 11

You are worthy and deserving of all that is coming to you.

You are stronger and braver than you think.

You are a powerful person with the world at your fingertips.

You have the power here and now to transform the direction of your life.

There is so much to look forward to.

January 12

You have the **power** to write your story, so make it a great one and dream big because you're the only one that can. No one else can dream your dream.

Think of your life as a movie, deciding which movie you would like to be in and which character you want to play, and have fun with it!

January 13

We all mess up sometimes.

Don't forget all the good things about someone because they made a mistake. Also, don't beat yourself up when you make a mistake.

Everyone is learning and growing.

January 14

Positive self-talk is the most important thing you can do to keep your happiness high. You can practice this throughout your day by repeating the following phrases.

- Today is a great day
- I love my life
- I'm so happy

Repeat these thoughts like a mantra in your mind to replace any negative self-talk you may be repeating to yourself.

January 15

Did you know it takes only 15 seconds to change a thought pattern?

If you have been feeling sad, angry, disappointed, or hurt, know that it's ok to have these feelings; they are **temporary** and will pass.

Remember just how wonderful and special you are.

January 16

Never stop dreaming.

Your dreams are a **preview** of what's to come.

If you can see it in your mind, you will hold it in your hand.

Dream more. Think less.

January 17

You are not constrained by who you think you are or who you have been in the past. That is the old you.

You can **instantly** transform into a completely different person with a new set of beliefs, ideas, lifestyle, and personality.

Nothing is permanent, so who do you want to be?

January 18

You are kind at heart.

You care about others.

You are a great friend.

You are a joy to be around.

When you feel anything other than this, the thoughts you are thinking about yourself are not in alignment with who you really are.

This is your reminder of just how wonderful you are.

Be kind to yourself today.

January 19

Have you taken a walk outside lately?

Walking outside in fresh air while gently moving your body is a great way to refresh and recharge yourself.

Just 15 minutes can give you a fresh outlook for the day, so give it a try.

January 20

When you speak your mind in the moment instead of staying quiet and letting your feelings build, you will find that your relationships will grow deeper.

When you are honest about your feelings, you allow others to give you what you need. Both parties will feel good and develop a deeper understanding of each other.

Honest and open communication is how we bond, and bonding with others is what we all desire deep down inside.

So, speak your mind today.

January 21

When you focus on what you share with others instead of your differences, you will find your relationships to become more meaningful.

January 22

Do you sometimes find yourself being lazy or procrastinating?

The good news is that you are not lazy. You are uninterested.

If you are struggling to start or finish something, let it go and spend your time doing something that **excites** you.

What excites you?

January 23

There is so much to look forward to, so **focus** your energy on your dreams and goals today. Forget about anything that may be bothering you.

Sometimes, we make things a lot harder than they need to be. You don't have to struggle to live your best life. Your dreams will be achieved effortlessly if you follow your instincts along the way.

January 24

Take some time to have fun today.

Stay present in the moment and enjoy this beautiful day.

Life can be so fun and adventurous if you just let it be.

January 25

Self-care is the key to feeling good and reaching your full potential.

When you take care of yourself, you are honoring yourself.

What are some things you can do for your self-care today?

Perhaps you could take a walk, enjoy a bath, eat a healthy meal, or simply say nice things to yourself and your body today.

January 26

Do you assume it was intentional when you are cut off in traffic?
It was most likely an accident.

When someone is rude, do you assume it was about you?
They were most likely having a bad day.

Try not to assume the worst. Accidents happen, bad days happen, and when you are having a bad day, a little understanding goes a long way! Remember this before you raise your voice.

This is your reminder to be kind and make good assumptions today.

January 27

Be brave and ask for what you want.

There are no limitations except the ones you make up in your mind.

Nothing is too big for you to achieve.

No goal is out of your reach.

The first step is to ask.

January 28

Don't worry about anything.

Relax and know that everything is working out for your highest good.

You are exactly where you are supposed to be, right here, right now.

January 29

Speak your mind today.

If something is bothering you, do you speak up?

When you want to speak your mind but decide to stay quiet to "keep the peace," you will feel uneasy inside and may even begin to resent the other party involved.

An issue that could be resolved with a few words can escalate into a huge drama in your head. Can you see where this has happened in your life?

January 30

Call a friend you haven't spoken to lately and say hi today.

Friendships are so important for your emotional health and well-being.

Sometimes we forget to reach out and say hello. This can lead to feeling disconnected from others.

You have many people who love and care about you, so who will you call today?

January 31

If you don't like something in your life, change it.

If you can't change it right away, change the way you look at it.

Remember that everything is **temporary**.

FEED YOUR SPIRIT

FEBRUARY

February is a month of cleansing. The second month of the year number two is the number that represents stability and balance.

Where can you bring more stability into your life? What do you need to cleanse out of your life? What bad habits can you drop? Healthier eating? More exercise? More nature? What can **nourish** you and help you grow into the person you want to be?

As you focus on visualizing what you would like to see, continue also inviting in your new life as you visualized last month. Keep your mind focused on what you want to create, and feel this energy as though it already happened.

Do the groundwork to build what you want to. Doubts may arise. Let them come and go and return to the knowledge that a life you can dream of **is** possible.

FEED YOUR SPIRIT

February 1

Be willing to move out of your comfort zone.

When you do this more often, you will start to experience life in a whole new way. You are always supported, no matter which direction you choose.

Try something new today!

February 2

Whatever is going on in your life, you have **created** it with your past thoughts and feelings.

To change how tomorrow looks, you must change the cycle of thoughts that loop in your head. Meditation and affirmations are a great place to start.

If you can identify a thought pattern that needs changing, for example, "I never have enough money," and start affirming a statement opposite to that, for example, "money comes easily," you will begin to change the cycle of thoughts that are preventing you from having all that you want.

You deserve to be happy.

You deserve to live your best life!

February 3

Did you know you have so many non-physical helpers ready to assist you whenever you need it, all you need to do is ask.

If you are feeling stuck, sad, disappointed, or need an answer to a problem, close your eyes and ask for a solution to be shown. Then somewhere along your day, you will be given what you need.

February 4

You are loved and protected.

Expect the unexpected today.

Lots of great things are on their way to you.

February 5

Today, think of something that helps you recharge and make a point to take some time out to do it. Even just 15 minutes will make a difference.

Sometimes we say to ourselves, "I don't have time," but this is not true.

There is always time.

You will find that when you take time to recharge, the time you spend doing other things throughout your day will be more focused and productive.

February 6

You can always turn a negative situation into a positive one.

It doesn't matter where you are, what is happening around you, or what has happened in the past.

Your mind and your intentions can take you anywhere you want to go.

Imagine the situation to be exactly as you want it to be.

Imagination is the key to all it is that you want and can transform anything you are dealing with in an instant.

February 7

Is your energy focused in one direction, or are you all over the place?

When you **focus** clearly on one defined outcome placing 100% of your energy on how to get there, this will be a lot more powerful than splitting energy into multiple goals.

For example, if you have a store, and say I want to sell teapots, seminars, green juices, and vitamins, then work on each item and how to sell it. This is split energy.

If you say, I want to make $100,000 per month selling natural products. This is a goal focused in one direction.

When you focus on one clear goal and put 100% of your attention into this goal, you will find it's simpler to achieve.

Your inspiration will be greater, you won't feel overwhelmed, and the results will be far better than you ever imagined.

February 8

Take one step at a time.

Everything is working out for you.

Be patient and enjoy the journey.

February 9

When you laugh and smile often, you invite more fun into your life.

When you are loving, you attract loving friends, family, and lovers.

When you complain, you invite more to complain about.

Every emotion you feel attracts more of the same to you.

Start to send out what it is you wish to receive.

February 10

Be kind to yourself today.

Maybe this means limiting how often you criticize yourself.

Become aware when you self-criticize and take a moment to remind yourself just how wonderful you really are.

You are doing great.

You are on the right track, and there is nothing for you to worry about. Everything is working out for you.

February 11

You are **worthy** of all the good that is coming to you.

You deserve to be happy and have all your dreams fulfilled.

There are no limits to what you can be, do or have.

February 12

Put yourself first!

It's ok to say no to events.

It's ok to ignore the phone if you don't feel like talking.

It's ok to leave behind old friends and start new friendships.

It's ok to do anything you want to do that makes you happy.

If it makes you happy, say yes. If not, say no guilt-free.

With every decision you make, do what it is you really want to do.

You are not obligated to anyone or anything, and you don't owe anyone anything, especially your precious time.

Spend your time wisely doing what makes **you** happy.

February 13

When you feel grateful for all that you have in your life, you will attract more to be grateful for. Feeling gratitude for what you have right now is a great way to shift your mood from negative to positive fast!

What are you grateful for today?

February 14

When you are excited about what you do, your time will fly by quickly.

When you are not excited, you will procrastinate.

If you find yourself procrastinating about doing anything, don't beat yourself up for - not getting it done. It is simply not what you are supposed to be doing at this time.

February 15

Relax, recharge, and unwind today.

When you are calm and relaxed, your head will clear, you will make better decisions, the people you **attract** into your life will align with your best self, and you will feel great!

February 16

If you find you are making commitments to yourself or others that you can't finish, this will be a good moment to evaluate why.

Then choose a different path and say no next time to anything you have identified as not right for you.

February 17

When you take the time to keep your thoughts positive, you will begin to receive only positive experiences.

Today, say to yourself, "everything is working out for my highest good," repeat this often to help shift your mindset.

February 18

Sometimes when things around you seem chaotic, what is really going on is the breaking down of old patterns.

The chaos around you is your life **shifting** into something new.

Remember everything you want when this happens, and focus your energy on what's to come.

February 19

Let go of what is in the past. Those experiences are behind you.

When you choose to spend your time appreciating what is **here** and **now**, the things you attract into your life will be even better than you imagined.

Appreciate more, live in the moment more, and think less!

February 20

Do what you love!

If you want to be successful with any goal in your life, the simplest way to achieve this success is to do what you love.

When you do what you love, success is easy. You will naturally align with the right people who can help, you will easily find solutions when obstacles arrive, and you will enjoy yourself every step of the way!

February 21

Relax and know that everything you want is on its way.

Relax and know that you can handle anything that comes your way.

Relax and know that you are fully supported and loved.

Relax and **remember** who you are.

You have more talent than you realize, more assistance than you ask for, and you can do so much more than you think is possible.

February 22

Past experiences can only affect you if you keep reliving them, so when you think about the past, be **selective**.

Holding on to any disappointment, sadness, or regret from the past will bring more of the same to you. Learn your lessons from those experiences and let them go.

Everything is temporary, but sometimes we hold on to past experiences, making them permanent in our minds. Look back with joy and look forward to your future.

You are on the right path.

February 23

Forgiveness is a strong form of love in any relationship. It takes strength to say sorry, and it can be even harder to forgive.

Forgive someone today.

Set yourself free.

February 24

Visualization is one of the most powerful tools available to create a rapid change in your life.

If you spend just 15 minutes a day imagining you have everything you desire, this will be enough to start bringing those things to you.

Visualize more, worry less.

February 25

Send love to everyone you interact with today. There is no need to save up love like you're trying to retire on it. Give love away like you're made of it.

Send out love to your family, your friends, your co-workers, your house, your car, your bed, your phone, your pets, and anything or anyone you interact with as you go about your day.

Love is the highest vibrational frequency.

When you are aligned with this frequency, your health and relationships will improve, you will feel more confident, have more energy, feel happier, and lots of love will flow back to you.

February 26

Look back at the past with gratitude.

No matter if your past feels positive or not so nice, you have learned and grown from it all.

February 27

If something is no longer right for you, walk away.

As you learn to put yourself first, walking away will become easier.

The faster you walk away from what is not right, the faster you will move into what is right for you. Walking away creates the space for new things to come into your life.

February 28

When making decisions, always **trust** your gut.

When you trust your gut instinct, you will make a decision that is correct for you. This decision will be aligned with everything you have been asking for and are moving towards.

If you are unsure of which direction to choose, meditate first.

Meditation will help you to tune into the higher part of yourself that knows the answer and will help you receive this clarity.

February 29

One positive thought turns into another, which turns into another.

One negative thought turns into another, which turns into another.

If you catch yourself in a negative thought spiral, notice it, then flip the switch. Replace those thoughts with something positive, such as listing things you are grateful for.

You control the direction of your thoughts.

Stop thinking by default. Take charge of the thoughts you think, and in doing so, you are taking charge of your life.

FEED YOUR SPIRIT

MARCH

The first month of Spring is the month of renewal, rebirth, and freshness.

In nature, as the season changes, the days get longer, with more light coming in. We are beginning to come out of the cold, waking from the hibernation of winter. Nature is a reflection of us, and if we align with its movements, we can flow with it in a similar way.

The equinox, which happens on March 21, symbolizes new light, new beginnings, and a new period of **growth**. It is also a time of hope, as with the freshness, we are reminded that things can be reborn, no matter what has happened in the past.

Don't let any thoughts of the past hold you back from what is possible in the future. Keep faith and hope in the life you have already begun to imagine.

This is the start of an upturn in the year, with more **optimism** and better and lighter times ahead. After visualizing what you wanted in the first two months of the year, you will see some seeds start to blossom.

FEED YOUR SPIRIT

March 1

A great time to **visualize** is while taking a walk. Give it a try for 15 minutes today. Simply walk around while picturing everything you want as if you already have it.

Perhaps visualization walks could be a new fun daily activity for you!

March 2

Every problem has a solution.

When you encounter a problem, think about what the best outcome would be, then focus 100% of your energy on this desired outcome.

Every experience is an opportunity to learn and grow, including any issues you may face.

March 3

Put yourself first today.

If this means canceling plans or saying no to something you don't want to do, do this for yourself guilt-free.

When you put yourself first, you will feel happier. When you are happier, you will naturally help others around you feel happy too.

March 4

Go for **everything** you want.

Regretting not trying is more painful than trying and things not working out as you expected. Just go for it!

You have nothing to lose and everything to gain.

March 5

When you are willing to forgive, your healing process begins.

Allow the love from your heart to wash over any old hurts, and know that you are worth healing.

March 6

You are never too old, too poor, or too busy to set a new goal.

There are so many great new experiences for you out there.

Setting a goal is an intention for change and is the first step to transforming your life path. You get to decide where you want to go next.

Make a list today. Put it in writing and make it official.

You're off to great places.

Today is the day!

March 7

Life is supposed to be fun!

What are the things you like to do for fun?

Have you been doing these lately?

Take time out to do something fun today.

March 8

Be **confident** in who you are and know your worth.

You are an amazing person with so many wonderful gifts to share with the world. It's your time to shine.

Have confidence in your direction.

Relax, trust, and know that you are worthy to receive all that you are asking for. You are doing great.

March 9

Well-being is constantly **flowing** to you.

If you are not noticing this to be true for you, something you are doing is blocking the flow, such as negative thoughts or ideas.

If this is true for you, today will be an excellent time to start a daily meditation practice. As you meditate, you clear your thoughts and allow space for your well-being to flow.

March 10

Are you nurturing your friendships?

Friendships come in many forms. You can have great friendships with your co-workers, family, or even the people you have known since childhood.

Great friendships have a huge impact on your happiness, well-being, and enjoyment of life, so take time to nurture the friendships you have now.

March 11

Today is going to be an incredible day!

Be ready for surprises and fun interactions with others to flow into your life as you go about your day.

March 12

Holding on to grudges does not serve you.

Today is a good day to practice letting go.

Think about any grudges or unresolved hurts you may have. Write them down in a list and take some time to do this.

Once these are identified, relax and take a deep breath in, and as you breathe out, intend to let them go.

Do this for a few minutes and repeat this process until you feel you have released these old thoughts that are no longer serving you.

March 13

Believe life is easy, and it will be.

Believe people are nice, and they will be.

Believe in yourself, and you will achieve everything you wish for.

What do you believe in?

March 14

Feeling happy **now** is the fastest way to bring everything you want into your life.

A great way to feel happy now is to focus solely on all the good things you have in your life. There are so many.

As you go about your day, identify everything you are grateful for and give thanks for them to yourself or out loud.

If you focus 100% of your energy on gratitude for even a day, you will rapidly change your thoughts to a happier mindset.

March 15

Your happiness does not depend on what others do or what you have.

Your happiness is created by the thoughts you think and your outlook.

The greatest gift you can give to yourself and your loved ones is to be happy. Your happiness is contagious.

March 16

How much time have you spent on yourself lately?

Are you taking time out for self-care, or are you constantly doing something or another throughout the day?

March 17

A simple act of kindness can change someone's day and even the direction of their entire life.

Be kind to everyone you meet today.

March 18

You can have everything that you want and can change your life in an instant. You are **worthy**, and the time to receive everything you want is now!

What are you waiting for?

You are the star of your movie.

Which movie do you want to create?

March 19

You don't need to be richer, thinner, or anything else to be happy now.

When you choose to see the positive in everything you have right now and are grateful for this very moment, you will find your true inner happiness.

What are you grateful for today?

March 20

Free yourself from other people's expectations.

The only obligation you ever have is to yourself.

Live your best life and do what makes you happy, no matter what.

Free yourself now by letting go of any person, situation, or commitment that brings you down or is not in alignment with who you are.

March 21

Release all your fears of worries and let go of what you cannot change.

Life is supposed to be fun.

Enjoy the ride.

March 22

Know what you want.

Know it's on its way, and know that you are worthy to receive all the good coming your way.

If you are not excited about what you are doing, it is most likely not the correct path for you at this time.

Move away from what does not excite you and towards what does.

Your inner guidance system is showing you the way.

Are you listening?

March 23

Every challenge in your life makes you stronger.

You never lose. You always win.

Everything is just as it's supposed to be, right here, right now.

There is no such thing as a loss, just a lesson learned.

Take the lesson and move forward.

March 24

When you feel tired or unmotivated, it's time to regroup and schedule some time for yourself. Take this time for yourself guilt-free.

During this time, do something that helps you to **recharge**.

If you are unsure what to do, think about the last time you felt great.

What were you doing? Do that!

March 25

Everything you are living **reflects** your past thoughts and feelings.

If nothing is changing, perhaps you're thinking the same thoughts over and over again. Notice this.

When you identify this pattern, you can catch and change repetitive thoughts that stop you from moving forward.

Only then will you have control over how the future looks for you.

March 26

It's perfectly **ok** to feel sad, angry, frustrated, anxious, or annoyed.

Having feelings doesn't make you a negative person. It makes you human!

Instead of fighting these feelings, notice them without self-judgment and let them go. These feelings are temporary. They don't define who you are.

March 27

Your energy is filled with light and inspiration.

It is time to stand up and be **proud** of who you are, what you want, and your goals in life.

You can and will achieve what it is that you desire.

Believe in yourself and your abilities.

March 28

Trust your gut with all decisions you need to make.

Forgive yourself for any mistakes you think you've made, and be grateful for what's to come.

Life is good!

March 29

When there is something you really want in your life, say to the universe.

"You know what I want. Send it to me the easiest way possible."

Then relax and let it go.

If you can do this with pure **trust** that what you are asking for will be delivered to you, it will be delivered faster than you think.

March 30

Stress begins with one negative thought.

If you allow it to continue, more and more of the same thoughts appear.

No matter how stressed you are feeling, you can turn it around in an **instant** by focusing on all the positive aspects of your life.

March 31

When you don't need anyone or anything to change for you to feel good, you are truly free.

FEED YOUR SPIRIT

APRIL

April continues with the momentum of spiritual renewal and growth. This is a great time to focus inward on your spiritual journey exploring and deepening the connection with your higher power.

April is a month of rebirth and **transformation**. As nature comes back to life, with flowers blossoming, this is a reminder of the cycle of life and the potential for renewal and growth. Now is the time to create positive change restoring a sense of balance and harmony. It's time to continue watering your flowers to ensure they grow.

Keep your mind healthy as it listens and responds to you.

In this period, you can feel increasing love and beauty around you as all warms up and gets brighter and more colorful. Allow this to reflect in you and your colors to come out. Get out and immerse yourself in it and let the beauty outside bring beauty and joy into you.

As you bring more joy into yourself, you can be a **light** to others. Isn't it amazing to be an example for others and show them the light on the path?

FEED YOUR SPIRIT

April 1

If you knew just how special you are, you would never doubt yourself.

There are ten great things you could focus on today, and also, there are ten negative things you could focus on.

Where are you focused?

April 2

When your energy aligns with another, you become extroverted.

When your energy is misaligned, you become introverted.

Pay attention to how you feel around others.

April 3

When you are kind to others, you help them to feel good.

When you help another feel good, they will be kind to others.

This is how energy is shifted, one person at a time.

April 4

Do you realize just how special you are?

You are doing so much better than you know.

You have helped more people than you realize.

You are closer than you think!

April 5

Life is a mirror. What you give out, you receive back, and you will receive more than you gave!

Here is how you can play with this.

Let's say you are feeling unloved. Send out lots of loving thoughts to everyone around you. This can be friends or strangers.

If you are feeling poor, buy someone a coffee or something small.

If you feel hurt or betrayed by a friend. Be a great friend to someone else.

Wherever you feel a sense of lack in your life, make an intention to give this out to someone today.

April 6

You have so much love and support. You are on the right path and don't need to worry about anything.

Take a breath, relax, and know that you are loved and supported today.

April 7

Did you know that by simply feeling gratitude for 15 minutes a day, you will boost your immune system, self-esteem, and overall happiness?

What are you grateful for today?

April 8

Great relationships begin with healthy communication.

When you communicate honestly and openly with others, you inspire them to do the same. Healthy communication helps you to develop deeper bonds with your friends and loved ones.

Be open, be honest, and be brave.

April 9

Love Is the highest frequency you can vibrate in.

When you feel love, you have reached the highest state of consciousness.

Love comes in many forms. Love can be romantic and can be felt for friends, family, pets, or even physical items and experiences.

When you feel the pure frequency of love, you will enter a state of natural happiness, gratitude, and oneness.

Love is simple to **create**, and it starts with you. Send out love to everyone and everything you interact with today. It's that simple!

April 10

You are a natural giver.

You naturally uplift all those around you.

The more you take time to feed your spirit, the more you have to give.

You are doing great!

April 11

Life is a dream.

You have the **power** to create your dream any way you wish.

What do you want to be, do or have?

Hold that image in your mind.

Never allow yourself to doubt.

Build your dream in your mind and expect everything you are asking for.

The best is yet to come.

April 12

Be happy now.

Be grateful now.

Feel good now.

There is no better time to start than right here, right **now**.

April 13

Life is too short to regret the past or any perceived mistakes.

Count your blessings, value your loved ones, and move on to your next adventure with your head held high.

April 14

Sleeping is an excellent form of meditation.

After a night of rest, you are starting a fresh new day, and you can decide to bring only the positives of yesterday forward.

Setting intentions before bed is a great way to wake up refreshed. Before going to bed, intend to have a great night's sleep, and you will.

April 15

Expectation is a powerful force that delivers what you want into your life.

Expect great things.

April 16

Every time you feel good or grateful about something.
You are saying yes to more of that.

Every time you complain about something.
You are saying yes to more of that.

Pay **attention** to what you are creating in your life.
You are creating it all with your thoughts and feelings.

Once you truly understand this, you will realize you have the world's power at your fingertips. You can create anything you want or desire. You can live the life of your dreams, and you should have it all.

You need to pay attention to what you are sending out.

April 17

There is a big difference between trying to make something happen and allowing it to happen.

When you feel relaxed, happy, or excited, you are allowing.

April 18

Being a part of a family is incredibly special.

Your family teaches you your most important life lessons.

Send love and gratitude to your family today!

April 19

Before making any big decision, make sure you are feeling good.

If you are not feeling good, take the time to feel better first.

When you are in a calm and relaxed headspace, the decision you will make will be right for you, so it's essential to take this time.

April 20

Do not let the behavior, words, or drama of others destroy your inner peace.

You can't control other people's actions, but you can control your response to the situations around you.

Learn to walk away from people who do not bring you joy. It's your life, and you get to choose.

April 21

Do you sometimes worry about money?

Perhaps you have money and worry about security. Perhaps you don't have enough money and want to attract more to you.

It's easy to worry about money when your **focus** is not having enough.

It's easy to worry about money when you are afraid to lose it.

To change this feeling of not having enough, say, "I can afford that," to everything you see around you.

This will start to shift your thoughts and energy around money, allowing more money to flow to you.

April 22

If you ask a happy person for advice, it will be good.

If you ask an unhappy person for advice, it may not be so good.

However, do you know where the best place to get advice is?

It's **yourself**. You have all the answers!

Give this a try this today.

Ask for an answer and wait for it to be shown.

April 23

Every time your life changes, a new and different **version** of you emerges.

There is no need to be attached to who you think you are.

Go with the flow and embrace the new you that is unfolding.

The best is yet to come!

April 24

Sometimes it is ok to sit back, relax and do nothing.

If you need to recharge, give yourself that time.

When you take the time to recharge, you will be restored to the best version of yourself and will feel energized and motivated once again.

April 25

Everything in your life is unfolding just right.

There is nothing to look back on or fix. You are on the right path.

April 26

Being happy doesn't mean everything is perfect. It means you are **choosing** to see the positive in all around you.

Look around today and notice all the wonderful things you have in your life. You have so much to be thankful for.

April 27

When something does not work out the way you planned, take it as a **lesson** and move on.

Sometimes the path to what you want is different than expected, but trust that everything you want is coming to you.

Looking back, you will understand why things happened this way.

For now, **trust** the process.

April 28

A simple 15-minute walk is a great way to recharge your energy.

Take a walk, breathe the fresh air, look at the sky, appreciate the beauty all around you and listen to the bird's sing.

Life is beautiful!

April 29

When was the last time you laughed?

If you had to think about it, it's been too long.

Laughing is a great way to release stress, boost your immune system, and improve your mood. Laughter relaxes your whole body.

Life is better when you are laughing.

April 30

You have so many things to be grateful for.

Count your blessings today.

FEED YOUR SPIRIT

MAY

May signifies the movement in areas of spiritual growth and **renewal**.

We see the continued stepping into summer with more light, color, and growth. It's a time to reconnect with our inner wisdom to align with our soul's journey. This is a good time to nourish ourselves by practicing self-love and acceptance while honoring our physical and spiritual needs.

May also symbolizes prosperity and **abundance**. Do you want to invite in more abundance? Can you notice your own limiting beliefs on this? For example, when you say, "I can't afford this" or "If only I could have that," as though it is a distant reality. Those thoughts are not true.

If you can dream it, you can believe it.

Express gratitude for what you have right here, right now. See the abundance around you to help more to come into your life.

May brings a burst of energy to help us realize our dreams and wishes.

FEED YOUR SPIRIT

May 1

Confidence is attractive and draws others to you much more than your physical appearance.

You have every reason to be **confident**.

You are incredible, talented, beautiful, and kind.

Remember who you are!

May 2

To instantly calm your mind, take a few long deep breaths in and out.

Whenever you are feeling stressed or anxious, stop and breathe.

May 3

Whatever you do, be sure it makes you happy.

If a person or situation in your life is not making you happy, it may be time to move away to something new.

Put yourself first.

May 4

When you let go of limiting thoughts surrounding money, you will start to find opportunities instead of roadblocks.

Once you shift your perspective and begin to think thoughts such as, "money comes easily to me," money will start flowing more easily to you.

Start to shift any negative beliefs you hold about your financial situation.

You **deserve** to be financially comfortable.

May 5

You have full control of where your attention and energy are going.

Now is an excellent time to turn off the TV, take a social media break, avoid dramatic interactions, and focus inwards on peace and happiness for yourself and others.

May 6

The more you worry about something, the stronger it becomes.

Ignore the things that worry you, and they will lose their power and vanish.

May 7

You can't go back and change the past, but you can start a **new** beginning.

Let go of the past and look forward to what's on your way.

May 8

An amazing day begins with a positive, grateful outlook.

What are you grateful for today?

May 9

If you want others to treat you well, make sure to lead by example and take care of yourself. You set the standard for how others treat you.

Love yourself more today, tell yourself how great you are, and expect many wonderful interactions to follow.

May 10

The thoughts you are thinking are reflected back to you.

Send out happy thoughts, and you will receive more happiness in your life.

Your thoughts are **building** your next chapter.

May 11

Life is supposed to be fun!

Get out of your day-to-day routine.

Make a change.

Do something different, something that excites you!

May 12

Life is too short to regret the past or any perceived mistakes.

Count your blessings, value your loved ones, and move on to your next adventure with your head held high.

May 13

Leave what's comfortable and do what you are afraid to do.

The places you are afraid to go might be where your happiness lies.

Take the first step, and don't look back.

May 14

Sometimes it may seem that things are happening around you that you cannot control, but you can always control the direction of your attention and energy.

Focus more on what you want and all the wonderful things you have in your life. There are so many.

Keep your attention on the positive things you see around you, and choose to ignore whatever else comes your way.

May 15

Everything you do makes a difference.

You have lots of incredible gifts to share with the world.

Be brave and go for what you want in life.

The more you follow your passions, the bigger the difference you will make to yourself and others.

May 16

Great things may take time.

Keep going, even when you do not see immediate results.

If you are confident in your direction, be **confident** that results will be shown to you soon.

May 17

Enjoy yourself today.

No matter what is happening around you, you can always choose to make it a great day!

May 18

If things are not looking good, don't worry. They are getting better.

If things are looking good, they are getting even better.

Whatever you are feeling right now, know that everything is getting better for you right here, right now.

May 19

If somebody is bothering you, here's a quick solution.

For the next three days, morning and night, say, " I love and appreciate (name) because...."

Find three things to appreciate about the person, no matter how small.

If you do this for just three days, the relationship will shift so fast that you will think the other person has changed, but you did it all!

May 20

It's better to fail than to not even try.

Don't let fear hold you back, go for it!

May 21

Your mind believes everything you tell it. Remember this next time you have any negative or self-doubting thoughts.

You are perfect, just as you are.

Tell yourself this more.

May 22

When you are fearful, you are not in alignment with what your higher self knows to be true.

If you find yourself feeling fearful, take three long deep breaths, and say, "everything is working out for me," then intend to let it go.

Everything is working out for you.

May 23

When starting something new, **believe** and act as if you can't fail.

What would you do if you couldn't fail?

May 24

Holding onto resentments affects you and only you.

Today, identify and let go of any negative feelings you hold over past situations, think of them as a lesson and intend to let them go.

May 25

When you are grateful for what you have in your life, you invite more of the same to come to you, for example.

If you give a gift to someone, and they are ungrateful, it's not likely you will do the same again.

If you give a gift to someone, and they are happy to receive it, you will be inspired to keep giving.

Think of gratitude in your daily life this way. The more grateful you are, the more the universe wants to give to you!

May 26

Expect good things to come.

Expect your every need to be met.

Expect the best.

May 27

Everything you are living reflects your past thoughts and feelings.

If nothing is changing, perhaps you're thinking the same thoughts over and over again. It's time to change the script.

May 28

Whatever you do, be sure it makes you happy.

If something doesn't make you happy, move on to something new.

When you are happy, you help to shift not only yourself but also everyone around you. Happiness is a gift.

May 29

You are amazing. Believe in yourself.

You have the power to create anything you want in your life.

What is it that you want?

May 30

Today, think of all the wonderful things you have to be grateful for. This could be your bed, your work, your friends, the sound of the birds, or a simple cup of coffee.

Whatever you experience today, say thank you.

May 31

You are loved.

You are supported.

You have the world at your fingertips.

JUNE

Now that we are fully into the summer. We can feel the inner **power** and brightness expanding within us. The joy, love, and gratitude are getting stronger.

June is named after Juno, the Goddess of marriage and love. Love is not just something directed at a person or felt for a moment. It is a state of being in everything and everywhere.

Can you feel the **love** in everything? Can you feel it in yourself? June is also the month when the roses bloom and are in abundance. The beauty of the rose is a great way to tap into the vibration of beauty. Let this feeling feed your spirit.

It is also an excellent time to put yourself out there. Don't wait for your life to improve but take action for it to happen. Have **confidence** in yourself, go for what you want, and speak your truth.

You are as worthy as anyone, **now** is the time for your voice to be heard.

FEED YOUR SPIRIT

June 1

Getting outside in nature is a great way to recharge your spirit.

Taking a simple walk while listening to the sounds of nature is a great place to start. Give it a try today.

June 2

Today, be thankful and think about how rich you are with all the wonderful friends and family you have in your life.

Loving and being loved is priceless. Enjoy your loved ones today

June 3

Are you spending your time looking forward to what the future holds or looking back with regrets?

You cannot change the past, but you can create your future.

Look ahead.

June 4

You are never stuck. Your life can change in an **instant**.

The more you feel stuck, the more time you need to spend imagining a different version of yourself.

Imagination is the key to all that you want.

June 5

When you empty your mind, you create space for new ideas and inspirations to flow. Simply closing your eyes and taking a few long slow deep breaths is a great way to start.

Repeat as needed.

June 6

Spend your time around people who bring you joy. Perhaps there is an old friend you could reconnect with today or a new friendship that you can start to build.

June 7

Your intuition is the greatest tool you have. Are you listening?

Let's say you are invited to dinner and don't feel like going but say yes because you think you should. This is an example of not following your intuition.

Your intuition is guiding you to all that you are asking for.

Trust yourself more.

Say yes when it feels right, and don't be afraid to say no.

June 8

Nothing is interesting to you if you are uninterested.

Keep your focus on the things that **excite** you the most.

June 9

When you choose what makes you happy, you will find that the other things you want will naturally fall into place.

What makes you happy?

June 10

No matter what you are going through, you can always turn a negative situation into a positive one.

There is always a light at the end of the tunnel.

Stay strong and believe in yourself.

June 11

Give out some love today, and it will be returned to you.

Love your bed, love your home, love your friends, love your body, love your life!

June 12

Focus on everything with gratitude and if there is a situation in your life where you can't feel grateful at all, spend extra time trying to get there.

This will help you move to your new chapter, more than you know.

June 13

There is no need to be stressed about anything. Everything is working out for you. Relax and enjoy your day.

June 14

It's never too late or the wrong time to change directions and build a completely new version of yourself.

Think of your life and past experiences as a training ground. You are never starting from 0 when you change directions. You take all your experience and wisdom with you into your next adventure.

So, what's next for you?

June 15

Do you catch yourself using certain words or phrases a lot?

Recognizing habitual thought patterns and replacing them with something new is a great way to positively change your life.

Recognizing this about others can also give you peace of mind that their words or opinions have nothing to do with you.

June 16

As the world around you changes, life may look uncertain. Trust the flow and know that everything is working out for you.

June 17

Children live in the moment and are full of natural joy. This is because they don't have years of mental baggage holding them back.

What mental baggage are you holding onto?

Let it go today.

June 18

The greatest gift you can give to yourself and your loved ones is to be happy. Happiness is contagious, and it spreads to everyone around you.

Your happiness does not depend on what others do or the things you have. It's created with the thoughts you think.

A quick way to increase your happiness is to think positively about everything and everyone around you. Give it a try today.

June 19

When was the last time you had fun?

If you have to think about it, it's been way too long.

Schedule some time for fun today!

June 20

Do what makes you happy, and the rest will follow.

You deserve to be happy; you deserve to be happy now.

June 21

Your time is precious.

Spend more time with the people you love, doing what you love to do, or one day you may wake up and say, "where did the time go?"

June 22

Know that you are great and try to care less about other opinions. The only person you need to impress is yourself.

You are amazing! You have a kind heart and have so much to offer the world, don't ever doubt yourself.

June 23

You are a unique person with **unlimited** potential.

You are worthy of all that is coming to you, and you are so blessed.

June 24

Have you ever tried being nice to someone who is rude to you? Instead of two people walking away feeling bad, both will feel uplifted.

While this may not be your normal response, and may not feel natural, give it a try and see how **you** control the direction of the energy, not them!

June 25

Your life isn't supposed to be the same every day. You are here to learn, grow and have many different life experiences, which is impossible if you let yourself get stuck in a rut.

Don't let money, status, or commitments hold you back from new things you want to try. If you are bored and need a change, take a chance!

June 26

Every possible version of your life is available for you to shift into. The happy you, the successful you, the fun you, so, who do **you** want to be?

June 27

Changing your thoughts and breaking habits of thought takes practice, just like learning to walk or drive a car.

This may not seem easy at first because you are retraining your habitual patterns, but if you stick with it, your thoughts will start to become positive without even trying. Just like driving a familiar route in your car, you have practiced so much that it comes naturally.

Sometimes when you try to release a pattern, you may notice things getting worse, but don't worry, this is temporary and is showing you the situation is beginning to shift. Keep going.

June 28

Success is not final, and failure is not final.

There is no final destination, so whatever you choose to do, make sure you are having fun along the way.

June 29

You are never too old to start something new. You are never too broke to make money. You are never too uneducated to start on a new path.

You **can** do, be and have anything you want in life.

Believing in yourself is the first step.

June 30

You came here to experience everything you want to experience. There are no limits except the limits in your mind. The only one stopping you is you.

There has never been a better time to make positive changes in your life than now. The time is **now**.

Intend to take a chance, and go for what you want, then a path will be shown, and you will know what to do next and how to get there.

Are you ready?

FEED YOUR SPIRIT

JULY

As we move into July, this is a great time to focus on having fun! Don't take yourself or life too seriously. This month holds a great opportunity for you to grow and remember to **enjoy** the journey.

In the heart of summer, we can also feel the warmth, and it's a time to play, be outdoors and enjoy your time.

In the sign of cancer, it's a time for connecting with family and friends, building relationships, and nurturing yourself. Love and relationships can move forward this month. Communicating clearly to yourself and others will help.

What and how do your ideal relationships look like? What type of connections are missing from your life? Can you open your heart and invite these in?

Know that you are **worthy** of all that you desire, and you are an extremely powerful being. Let the feelings of fun feed your spirit this month, as in the spirit of fun, we can attract more joyful experiences effortlessly. Most importantly, enjoy the journey.

FEED YOUR SPIRIT

July 1

There is a difference between a gut feeling that something is wrong for you and a gut feeling of fear.

Learn to identify the difference so you do not walk away from great opportunities because your gut tells you so. This may be fear holding you back.

July 2

When was the last time you had fun and laughed?

Laughter relieves stress, improves your mood, and it increases your happiness and well-being.

Do something that makes you laugh today, such as chatting with a friend or watching a funny movie. Whatever it is that makes you laugh, do this!

July 3

When you focus on problems, you will find more problems.

When you focus on opportunities, you will find more opportunities.

When you focus on joy, you will find more joy.

What are you focusing on?

July 4

You don't have to change anything about yourself to please another.

It doesn't matter what others think of you. It only matters what you think of yourself.

Live the life you truly want to live.

Live free!

July 5

Make your decisions based on if you **want** the experience, not based on if you can afford it or not. Once you have decided what you want, a way will be shown to you.

If you say, "I can't afford it," you close the door.

Instead, say, "how can I afford it?"

July 6

Always trust your instincts. This is the universe talking to you, letting you know which direction to move.

If you feel it, follow it, don't let your head get in the way.

Trust your intuition first.

July 7

It's a beautiful day. It's a new day, and with every new day comes a fresh start, new ideas, and a new **version** of you.

July 8

Something wonderful is going to happen today.

Can you feel it?

July 9

Your parents gave you life and gave the most they had to offer, even if sometimes it did not seem like enough.

As an adult, you have all the tools you need to live a happy and enriching life. When you blame or hold resentment towards your parents, you also give yourself an excuse not to be your best self.

Send some love to your parents today, forgive any resentments you may hold towards them, and remember that nothing from your past can affect you today.

July 10

No matter what is going on in your life, know that **you** have the power to create any life you want in an instant.

You hold all the power!

You are the magician, writing the story of your life. You do this with your thoughts, feelings, and expectations.

If you say people are unkind, they will be.

If you say you never have enough money, you will never have money.

If you say you are unlovable, love won't come.

Know that you are creating it all.

Believe you can change it. Believe it can happen in an instant.

And, most importantly, believe you are worthy.

July 11

A difference of opinion is never a good reason to lose a friend. If someone drops your friendship because you have different views or ideas, they were not your friend to begin with.

Also, if you have a good friend who doesn't think the same way as you, **accept** your differences, and enjoy the friendship you have.

July 12

Your emotions are always offering you guidance.

Are you listening?

Try not to ignore your feelings. Instead, embrace them and let them guide you into the life that's waiting for you. If it feels bad, move away. If it feels good, move towards it.

July 13

You are perfect just as you are, don't let your mind tell you otherwise.

July 14

There are no limits. There are only limits in your mind. The fastest way to remove limiting thoughts is to imagine what you want without thinking about how you will get there.

Every accomplishment began with the decision to try.

What will you try today?

July 15

Sometimes we become so caught up in our day-to-day life we forget that what's most important is to be happy.

This is your reminder to do something that makes you happy today.

July 16

You can walk away from friends, but it's not so easy to walk away from family members, which is why family can be our biggest challenge.

But remember, while you may have many ups and downs, you learn so much from your family. They are here to teach you.

July 17

Never worry about what someone is thinking about you. You can never know what anybody truly thinks, so why worry about it?

Sometimes we worry so much about what others think of us that we don't live our lives in the way that serves us best.

It's the thoughts we think about ourselves that can be the most damaging of all. Speak to yourself with kindness.

Focus in, not out. Please yourself first.

July 18

Your emotions are always offering you guidance.

There is no need to discount your feelings. Instead, embrace them and let them guide you into the life that's waiting for you.

July 19

Sometimes when you're feeling drained and tired, drinking lots of water will help. Water will recharge you more than you realize.

Give it a try.

Drink lots of water today!

July 20

When things are happening that seem out of your control, let those things go and focus on an entirely new subject.

Perhaps thinking about all the new experiences you would like to have. This would be a great place to start.

July 21

If you are inspired to do something, act **fast**!

There is no need to overthink something that feels right. This will lead to confusion and procrastination instead of the action you are being called to.

July 22

If you enter a room full of angry people, you will start to feel angry.

If someone gives you a compliment, you will feel good.

If someone honks at you while driving, you will get annoyed.

Do others hold this much power over you? Only if you let them.

You can keep your energy high at all times, not only for yourself but for others. This is the most important thing you can do right now!

When you **consciously** do this and choose to be a positive light, especially when others are not in a good place, you show them the way. Then the next person does the same, and the next, and the next. It's like a positive wave that keeps spreading.

July 23

Music has the ability to completely shift your energy.

Listen to some music that makes you feel happy today.

July 24

There is no need to deny any emotions.

If you are angry, be angry. Feeling sad? be sad.

Feel your emotions fully, then let them go to shifting your focus onto what it is you really want.

July 25

Gratitude is one of the most **powerful** tools you have to start attracting everything you want into your life.

What are you grateful for today?

July 26

Spending some time in nature can shift your energy fast.

Simply getting outside for 15 minutes and listening to the sounds around you while being present in the moment will help you to feel great.

July 27

Everyone struggles at some point, and that's ok.

We are all on a journey.

Enjoy the journey.

July 28

Children laugh and play often. They are our teachers, reminding us of who we are and what we've forgotten.

When was the last time you laughed and played?

What makes you laugh? What do you enjoy? Spend more time doing that!

July 29

Never regret anything in your life.

The past is over, and the only power it holds over you is the attention you give to it. **Decide** to let it go now.

Take the lessons from your past, forgive yourself for any perceived mistakes, and focus forward on all the good that is coming to you.

July 30

Negative thoughts are a habit.

Positive thoughts are a habit.

A habit is a system of repetition.

You can easily break the cycle of negative, self-doubting thoughts by making positive thoughts a habit.

Repetition is the key!

July 31

Feel the energy of love.

Love does not have to be romantic. You can love your friends, family or pets, your job, desk or pen, and guess what?

When you send out loving vibrations, they are mirrored right back to you, and very soon, you will start to notice just how much love you have all around you.

AUGUST

Moving into Leo's energy, we might feel an action-orientated energy as the power of the lion can be felt. This is one of the most powerful times of the year.

Do you know how **powerful** you are? You have the power to direct your life as you want and make anything happen.

Find the **courage** to make the changes you want to make. Practice speaking to yourself with positive self-talk, reminding yourself of the strength and capacity you have. You can also use affirmations to help you and the quotes throughout this book to reinforce your self-confidence.

Leo is not afraid to be seen, so don't be shy. August is the number eight, which is also the symbol of infinity. This is You! An infinite, energetic being having a physical experience.

Although often, things happen that are not within your control, much of your life is within your control. You are the creator of your reality. Use this power to continue building what you have dreamed of.

FEED YOUR SPIRIT

August 1

The only obligation you ever have is to live your best life and to be happy.

Choose to be happy now by letting go of any person, situation, or commitment that brings you down, and do it guilt free!

Remember this and take action. Your time is now.

August 2

Life is really simple, but we tend to overthink and make things more complicated than they need to be.

Take a moment to focus inside and let your mind go quiet.

Smile and know it's going to be a fantastic day.

August 3

Make sure to encourage yourself when trying something new, saying things like "everything I do is a success" and "opportunities are everywhere."

Positive self-talk is essential to keep you excited and motivated.

What excites you?

August 4

Self-confidence is essential to truly live your best life.

Be yourself, have confidence in who you are, and most importantly, try not to seek the approval of others, as only **you** can know what's right for you.

August 5

When was the last time you said something nice about yourself?

Tell yourself great things today, such as "I am fun, happy, and beautiful" have fun with this!

August 6

Everything is working out for you.

You are on the right path, relax and **trust** the flow.

August 7

Making a decision that seems final can be hard, but what's harder is staying where you know you're not meant to be.

Have peace of mind knowing that no decision is final, so do what's right for **you** at this moment, and trust in what happens next.

August 8

A new day means a fresh new start.

Be **clear** about the things you want. When your thoughts are general and unfocused, they don't hold much power.

What do you want to accomplish?

Be clear.

August 9

You may feel uncomfortable speaking your mind, but it's more uncomfortable to hold on to resentment over unspoken words.

Communicate openly and honestly today.

August 10

Nothing is given to you that you can't handle.

You can handle more than you think.

Try not to sweat the small stuff today and make it a great one!

August 11

Only **you** know what is best for you.

Following your joy and intuition will guide you along your unique path.

Only you know the way.

August 12

You are kind.

You are uplifting to those around you.

You are fully supported with all you want in life.

You are loved!

August 13

Do you want to make a positive difference in the world?

Start with yourself first.

Do what you need to do to be happy. Only you know what changes need to happen for you to be truly happy.

Once your happiness bucket is full, you can start to help others with a kind word, a helping hand, or just being there, and you will have lots to give.

This is how you make a positive difference in the world.

August 14

Do you feel worthy of all the good that is coming to you?

If you find yourself stuck in situations that no longer serve you, perhaps you don't feel you deserve good things... But you do!

Everything you could ever want is here for you right **now.**

Now is the time to believe in yourself and feel deserving of what's to come.

You are so deserving of all the good that's coming your way.

Let it in!

August 15

A healthy outside starts from the inside.

Today, drink lots of water, get some fresh air, do something that will make your body feel good, and take some time for mental relaxation.

When your body and mind are healthy, your path will be clearer.

August 16

When you feel stuck, your work is vibrational, not physical.

Before taking any action, be sure to take care of your energy first. Take a walk, meditate or breathe in and out a few times. This will assist you.

August 17

If you are always trying to be "normal" and fit in, you may never discover just how amazing you really are.

You are capable of incredible things

What is it that you want?

Let your imagination guide you today.

August 18

There is no need to work harder or try harder.

Imagine and feel more into what you want, then you will enter a natural flow where everything good comes to you easily.

August 19

Are you happy with the work that you do?

Do you wake up excited to start the day or dread what's to come?

When you are blissful while working, your work life will improve.

Make small steps towards this by finding enjoyment in your work.

August 20

Success is not just getting everything you want. It's also enjoying the journey along the way.

Enjoy the journey.

August 21

Think about the moment you were born and your mother's immense love for you. She did the best for your health, spoke words of love, and had many sleepless nights just checking to see if you were ok.

Do you love yourself this much? It's time to start!

August 22

The longer you think a thought, the stronger it becomes.

Pay attention to your thoughts today.

When a negative or self-doubting thought appears, replace it with a positive statement, such as "everything is working out for me today."

August 23

There is no better time than **now** to start on a new path.

Today, identify one thing in your life you can let go of and one thing you want to begin. This is a great place to start!

August 24

Sometimes when things don't seem to go your way, this can be a great place to launch new ideas and plans for your life.

Inspiration and determination often come from struggle. If you can see it this way, you're one step ahead!

August 25

Good things happen, and bad things happen.

Where are you placing your attention?

Whatever you **focus** on grows.

Life will always have its ups and downs, but your attention determines where you go. Remember this and ignore anything that takes you on a path you are not interested in following.

August 26

Today, send invisible love to everyone you see.

This little shift in thinking can transform your whole day!

August 27

If you think something is nice about someone, be sure to tell them.

You will feel good, and you will help others feel good.

August 28

Every cell in your body responds to every thought you think. Remember to love your body today, especially sending good thoughts to any areas that are bothering you,

Love your body, every part of it, just as you are.

August 29

Today, remember a happy time in your life.

Remember every feeling and emotion. Imagine being there again.

Getting into this state of mind will help you attract more happiness.

August 30

Happiness starts with you. Not with your relationships, not with your job, not with your money, not with your circumstances, but with you.

August 31

When you are excited about something, working towards it will not feel like work, it will feel like fun!

If you are not excited, you will procrastinate.

If you find yourself procrastinating about doing anything, now will be a good time to change directions and move toward the things that excite you more.

What excites you?

SEPTEMBER

We are coming to the end of summer, and it is a great time to complete those projects and wrap up anything not yet completed.

We still have the mood of fun and play, so keep exploring what makes you **happy** and do lots of it! When you are happy, you are more likely to make others happy than if you are dull and gloomy.

This is also a powerful month for manifestation and the time for harvesting the crops, so you can now reap what you sowed in the earlier part of the year.

Are you ready to receive?

In order to receive, we need to keep our heart open and stay tuned to the vibration of love.

FEED YOUR SPIRIT

September 1

The only obligation you ever have is to live your best life and to be happy.

Choose to be happy now by letting go of any person, situation, or commitment that brings you down, and do it guilt free!

Remember this and act. Your time is now.

September 2

Getting outside in nature is a great way to recharge your spirit.

Taking a simple walk while feeling the energy all around you is a great place to start. Give it a try today!

September 3

Your emotions offer clarity.

Suppose you are stuck trying to make a decision or need to decide what path to choose. Imagine both paths and choose the one that feels better for you.

September 4

You are worthy.

You are perfect, just as you are.

You deserve to live your life with joy and fun.

Do something that makes you feel good today!

September 5

Everything you want is because you think it will make you feel good. If you feel good first, you will find that what you want will come to you faster than you know.

Think of your mind as a tool. You can retrain your mind into happier thoughts, which leads to a happier you.

September 6

Making a conscious effort to start your day with gratitude will help great things flow to you today.

What are you grateful for?

September 7

Is there someone in your life you can't forgive?

This is the person you need to let go of the most.

Forgive and let go.

September 8

Dare to be different, be authentic. Then it's impossible to lose.

Listen to your inner voice. It's the only truth.

September 9

Do you feel like you need a vacation or some relaxation?

You can take a mental vacation anytime you want by practicing meditation for just 15 minutes. Meditation is the simplest way to get the stress relief and relaxation you need.

September 10

Starting over gives you a chance to rebuild even better.

Where would you like to start over?

Start there.

September 11

Be kind, even when others are not, and before you know it, you will be surrounded by kind people. People change when you change.

September 12

Smile, and think about three great things in your life.

Really focus on this for a few minutes.

There is so much good all around you.

Pay attention to those things today!

September 13

You are perfect, just as you are.

Everything is working out for you.

You have lots of wonderful gifts to share with this world.

Never forget just how amazing you are!

September 14

Worrying is a waste of time, and it steals your happiness.

There is nothing for you to worry about.

Everything is working out for you.

Enjoy the journey, all of it.

September 15

If you need advice or feel stuck in some way, ask ~~your higher self~~ GOD for the answer before you go to bed. Really ask.

In the morning, you will receive clarity and know what to do next.

September 16

Did you know that taking a few deep breaths completely calms the mind?

As you go about your day today, stop periodically to take three long slow deep breaths in and out. Stay calm.

September 17

If something is going well for you, give it all your attention and focus. Be thankful and feel into the moment.

If something isn't going so well, take a walk, read a book, watch a movie, or do anything you can to forget about it.

September 18

It's not possible to feel good and bad at the same time, so when you are feeling bad, the quickest way to shift this is to think about something great.

Think about something great and focus on it for 17 seconds. That's all the time it takes to change your mood.

September 19

There is no such thing as failure. It's just a lesson learned.

Don't let any perceived failure stop you from moving forward, enjoy the lesson and look **forward** to what's next to come.

September 20

You came here for adventure.

You came here to explore.

You came here for fun!

September 21

Life is a mirror. What you give out comes back to **you**.

So, send out loving thoughts, be grateful for what you have, and say nice things to those around you, even if it doesn't come so naturally to you.

Start to shift the way you think, and before long, your life will be a complete reflection of what you have been sending out.

September 22

Are you holding on to anything that no longer serves you?

Let it go today.

September 23

Relationships help you to learn and grow.

As you improve your well-being and focus on positive things, you may find your relationships change.

Some relationships will fall away, some new ones will form, and the relationships that stay will become more joyful than they were before.

September 24

Healthy communication is the best way to form deep relationships.

Often, misunderstandings and negative feelings about others can easily be resolved by simply expressing how we feel.

Many of us find it hard to communicate openly, we have been trained to please people, but this pleases no one in the long run.

To deepen your relationships, you must be open and honest, even when it may be uncomfortable to do so.

September 25

It's better to make a mistake than to always wonder, what if?

Taking a chance is never the wrong thing to do, and there are no mistakes.

What you think of as a mistake is really a time for you to learn and grow on the way to your next step.

Take a chance.

September 26

How much time have you spent on your positive self-talk lately?

It doesn't take much time to **remind** yourself of how wonderful you are.

Here are five simple reminders to repeat throughout your day.

- I love my life
- I am amazing
- I can do anything
- I am talented
- I am loved

September 27

If you don't wish to be a part of something, simply don't give it any attention. Change the channel.

There is so much beauty and joy in the world. Focus there.

September 28

When you blame another, you are powerless.

Instead of blame, look inside to see what patterns you have that are attracting what you do not want.

You have the power.

September 29

Let go of all expectations.

The things you are asking for may not come in the way you expect.

Trust that you are moving in the right direction.

Trust that what is happening now is the right path for you.

September 30

You are the master of your life, and you choose which direction you go in with the thoughts you think.

You can have a happy life, a fun life, or a stressful life.

Nobody is responsible but you.

You hold all the power.

OCTOBER

The animal totem associated with the month of October is the falcon bird spirit. The spiritual meaning of the Falcon is a **balance** of mind, body, and spirit.

As winter approaches, we are beginning to return **inwards** after a summer of being out and about. We can return to introspection and quiet. When we take time to check in with ourselves, we can see if we are in balance on all levels.

Have you been looking after your body? Is your mind in a healthy state? Are your thoughts lifting you up or pulling you down? How is your spirit feeling? Do you feel connected to it?

Take this time to **connect** with yourself and see if there is anywhere you need some extra love and attention.

Get ready for a cozy, snug winter full of self-care, warmth, and love.

FEED YOUR SPIRIT

October 1

When you do what you love, others will love it too.

Not only that but people will be inspired to help you get where you are going. This will help you towards your success.

If you don't love what you do right now, find a way to make it feel fun!

The **faster** you can do this, the faster better opportunities will come to you, and there is no better time to start than right now.

October 2

The most important thing you can do for yourself is to do things that make you happy. Plan that trip, spend time with great friends, and find reasons to laugh often.

Most importantly, if something in your life doesn't make you happy, learn to let it go.

October 3

Send out loving thoughts, and you will receive more love in your life.

Whatever you are thinking is being sent to you.

It's all a reflection.

You matter, you are worthy, and you are loved.

October 4

A happy day begins with a happy mindset.

Create your day by thinking about all you have to be grateful for and make it a great one!

October 5

You are a natural giver.

The more you give to yourself, the more you have to give to others.

Fill your cup first.

October 6

You laughed, played, and enjoyed being in the moment as a child!

What happened to this child with a happy free spirit?

Perhaps you started caring about what others think a little too much or focused on troubles over enjoyment.

This is your reminder to play more, laugh more, and not care about what anyone else thinks along the way.

October 7

Do you believe you deserve good things?

Do you believe you are worthy?

If you don't, you won't allow yourself to have anything you want. You will find obstacles and roadblocks instead.

You deserve to enjoy a great life and have all your desires met.

You are worthy.

October 8

Take notice of old thought patterns that no longer serve you.

When you can identify this pattern, you can catch and change repetitive thoughts, and then you will have so much more control over how the future looks for you.

October 9

Today look in the mirror and say, "I am perfect, just as I am."

Every mirror you pass today, repeat this phrase, and before long, you will start to believe this truth.

October 10

It's fun to live in abundance, and **nothing** is stopping you!

Imagine spending lots of money, and you will attract more money to you.

Imagination is the key to all you are asking for.

October 11

We are all givers at heart. When someone asks for advice, we want to help, and when you are asking for advice, others will give it to you.

However, only **you** know what is right for you, so make sure to check in with yourself first before asking others.

You have more answers inside you than you realize, just ask (yourself), and you will receive the answers you need.

It will be shown to you.

October 12

Negative messages do not serve you in any way, do not pay attention to society's messages about what's expected of you.

You write the script for your life, don't live somebody else's script.

You get to choose.

October 13

While you can't always control what's happening around you, you have complete control over the thoughts you think.

Look for the positive.

October 14

When you give to others, it opens the door for you to receive.

Give something to someone today. This could be as simple as a cup of coffee or a compliment.

October 15

We can all feel uneasy or overwhelmed sometimes.

When this occurs, find ten things to appreciate about what is happening. Take your time to find ten. Writing them down is even better.

This will help the situation quicker than you know!

October 16

Nobody can ruin your day or put you in a bad mood unless you let them. It's up to you how seriously you take the behaviors and actions of others.

As you can't control what others do, let those moments pass, and return to your good feelings and thoughts!

October 17

What would you ask if you knew you could have anything you wanted?

Have you asked?

It can be easy to forget that you can have anything you want.

What's stopping you?

Intend to let any fears and doubts go today.

Give trust and expectation a try.

October 18

You are a natural giver.

You are a joyful person who brings happiness to those around you.

You are perfect, just as you are!

October 19

While foods may be "good" or "bad" for you, your thoughts about the foods you eat are much more powerful than what you ingest.

If you eat something you **believe** will benefit you, it will likely have that effect, and if you eat something you consider bad, it will likely make you feel bad.

No matter what you eat today, say, "this food nourishes me in a healthy way. I feel great."

This intention will help your body get the most out of what you eat.

October 20

You **deserve** to live a wonderful happy life. The simplest way to achieve this is to spend a little time each day tending to your happiness.

This can be done in any way that works for you, such as reading a great book, taking a walk, spending time with good friends, sitting in meditation, or simply reading these messages in the morning.

Tend to your happiness today!

October 21

Joy is your natural state of being. If you are miserable for any reason, this is most likely caused by the thoughts you are thinking.

Once you understand this, it will be easier for you to redirect your thoughts and find more joy in your life.

Look for the positive today. This is a great place to start.

October 22

You are amazing and more powerful than you think.

Ignore the voices in your head that tell you otherwise.

Make it a great day!

October 23

It takes repetition to learn a new language, and it takes repetition to change habitual thinking.

As you repeat positive statements, your mind will be trained into positive thinking, and it will begin to come naturally to you.

Keep going. You're doing great!

October 24

Do you make time for your friends, or are you always too busy?

Friendship and laughter are essential parts of a happy life.

Make time to nurture your friendships and have some fun!

October 25

Show some kindness to yourself today. This may mean limiting how often you criticize yourself.

Become **aware** of how you talk to yourself.

Be kind to yourself.

October 26

Love is the most powerful force in the universe, which is one of the reasons why falling in love feels so good.

To attract more love into your life, send invisible love to everyone and everything you interact with today.

October 27

Trust your instincts. Your instincts are guiding you.

Take a leap of faith today.

October 28

Focus on the positive aspects of everyone around you.

The more you focus on the positive aspects of others, the more positive aspects you will find.

You will be surprised to see how much another can shift when you shift how you think.

October 29

Holding onto grudges or old hurts doesn't serve you in any way. You are simply punishing yourself for someone else's actions.

Identify any negative feelings you may be holding on to and make a conscious effort to let them go today.

October 30

You are under no obligation to be the same person you were five years, five months or even five minutes ago.

Allow yourself to grow and change.

October 31

Love is a state of being.

Love is not outside of you, it is deep **within** you.

You can never lose it, and it cannot leave you.

You are loved.

FEED YOUR SPIRIT

NOVEMBER

As we continue the journey inward, we are taking this time to realign, refocus and reenergize ourselves. Rest is just as important as action.

If we overdo it, we will end up exhausted. Resting allows us to recuperate and **recharge** our energy so that we can give it our best when we return to productivity mode.

There is never any rush, so don't put pressure on yourself. Allow yourself this time. Also, as we **realign** with ourselves, remember that everything in the external is a mirror.

The external is a gift, helping you to see yourself. Be grateful for all you experience, and in that energy of gratitude, you will attract more positive experiences.

The time is here and **now**, in this present moment. Allow yourself to feel what you feel and be your true self now.

FEED YOUR SPIRIT

November 1

Your life is supposed to be fun, happy, and feel good.

It's impossible to control all your thoughts. Instead, you can guide them by reaching for a better feeling thought, again and again.

As you make this a daily habit, it will become easier for you.

November 2

If you don't brush your teeth every day, you may not notice the effects for a while, then one day, you will need a root canal and ask, "what happened?"

Keeping yourself in alignment should be thought of in the same way. If you don't make an active effort daily to stay positive and happy one day, you will wake up depressed and miserable and ask, "what happened?"

You are doing great! Stay on your positive path.

November 3

Happiness is not over there, yesterday or tomorrow.

Happiness is here and now.

November 4

Visualize for everything that you want, and practice gratitude for what you have in your life now.

This is the fastest way to rapidly transform your life!

November 5

Never doubt yourself.

You are more powerful than you think.

You are doing great.

November 6

Today, decide to have a great day and let your anticipation attract positive experiences into your life.

Expect only good things.

November 7

Take more time for the things you have been neglecting.

Think about the areas in your life you could start to rebalance and try to make more time for things you have been neglecting.

November 8

When you imagine others as their best version, you will bring out the best version of them. This is the version that will show up for you.

Instead of asking someone to change, imagine them at their best.

November 9

Sometimes you need to be alone.

Your alone time is the best time to connect to yourself without outside influences.

Here you will align with your intuition, and then, you will know what steps to take next.

November 10

When you find yourself worrying about something in your life, ask yourself if this will matter a month or a year from now.

Worries are temporary, so the best thing to do is to let them go.

Worry less and relax more today.

November 11

Take a chance today because you'll never know just how wonderful something could turn out to be.

If it is in your mind, it is calling you and is worth taking a chance for.

You have nothing to lose and everything to gain.

November 12

You **attract** what you think about into your life.

If you are fearful or worried about something, you are calling it towards you, and the same goes for your happy thoughts.

If you catch yourself in a negative thinking loop, try to shift to thinking about something good. The more you consciously make this shift, the easier it becomes.

November 13

It's never too late to change the course of your life.

You can build a completely new version of yourself anytime you wish.

You must first decide who you want to be.

November 14

Nothing that has happened in the past needs to affect you today.

Release the past with love.

Let it go.

November 15

Everything you are thinking is activating within you.

What is within you will show itself to you.

November 16

Set healthy boundaries.

Your time and energy are precious.

You teach people how to treat you by showing them what you will and won't accept. Only accept the best.

November 17

Life is all about balance.

You don't always need to be on the go.

Sometimes it's necessary to sit back, relax and do nothing.

November 18

Being in love is the most beautiful feeling in the world. It's not limited to romantic relationships. Find someone to fall in love with, a friend, a family member, or even better... Yourself.

November 19

Leave any bitterness or resentment you are feeling behind today, even if just for a moment. This is the beginning of freedom.

Making a conscious effort to identify and release these feelings will help you to think less of those thoughts in the future. Your mind won't be trained to go there anymore.

November 20

Don't worry about what others think of you, as many times, these thoughts are not only negative but very far from the truth.

People like you and think good things about you.

November 21

If your daily routine is the same day to day, and you are becoming uninspired, this is a normal reaction.

You thrive when you are growing.

Change up your routine.

November 22

Happiness is created by you, suffering is created by you, joy is created by you, and worry is created by you.

Don't give anyone credit for the good or the bad.

Speak your truth, speak of possibilities, speak of health.

What you speak of is what you have.

November 23

Love, enjoy and be thankful to your beautiful family today. They are here to teach us our most important lessons and are our greatest gifts, whether we realize it or not.

Be thankful for the people who love you, and enjoy this day!

November 24

Every time you are grateful, every time you appreciate something, every time you feel good about something, every time you love something, you are saying **yes** to more of this.

November 25

You are free.

You have value.

You are powerful.

You have a purpose.

You are loved.

November 26

Love is the most powerful healing energy.

Everything you do with love spreads joy and healing to yourself and those around you.

Send love to everyone around you today, even those who annoy you, for they may need it the most!

November 27

Offer no resistance to life, be in a state of grace and ease, and look at nothing as good or bad.

November 28

Gratitude can **transform** any situation.

When you are grateful, you shift your vibration, moving from negative to positive in an instant!

You have so much in your life to be grateful for.

November 29

Are you happy?

Do something that makes you happy today. If you can't quickly think of what this would be, take some time to remember what truly brings you joy.

Once you have identified what that is, schedule this time for yourself.

November 30

When you make a decision, follow it through quickly and as far as you can take it. Changing your mind sends out confusing signals. No dream or vision has time to grow in this space.

Make a decision that feels exciting, and go for it!

DECEMBER

In the depth of winter and the festive season, we can bring a sense of **joy** and celebration back in. Towards the end of this month, we are in linear time, closing out the year.

You may want to **reflect** on what you experienced over the past twelve months, noting the good and the bad, what you learned, and what you wish to grow more. When was your best moment? What made you happy this year? What are you happy that you achieved and want to do more of? Feel it, and let it fill you with that warm feeling.

Finish off the new year on a note of **gratitude** and with an appreciation for the good times, knowing that you can continue expanding on what you love.

Get ready to have an amazing year ahead and start it with clarity of knowing what you want to achieve, build, and manifest in the year ahead, knowing that you have the capacity and strength to make it happy.

FEED YOUR SPIRIT

December 1

You are in the perfect place for a fresh new start, and nothing needs to change around you for this to begin. Simply build the picture in your mind.

Imagine your life was perfect, and you had everything you wanted right here, right **now**. What does that life look like?

As you spend more time picturing this and less time worrying about what is happening now, your life will start to change faster than you realize!

December 2

Helping someone feel great is a wonderful way to help you feel great.

A simple way to feel better is to pick someone in your life and do something nice for them. A random act of kindness goes a long way.

This could be as simple as giving a compliment, buying a small gift, or helping with a task.

Try a random act of kindness today.

December 3

If you have a decision to make, always **trust** your instincts first.

When you let your intuition guide you, you can be sure you will be heading in the right direction.

Trust yourself!

December 4

Children are so full of joy, and you were just like that once, too, finding laughter and fun in everything!

Reconnect with your inner child today and make it a great one!

December 5

There is nothing you need to change about yourself.

You are perfect, exactly as you are.

Love yourself, accept yourself, and nurture yourself.

December 6

Is there something you want in life that you are not trying for because you don't believe it's possible?

Let your mind go free today and explore the feeling of having all your desires met. Imagine your life as you really want it to be.

Let your imagination be a preview of what's to come!

December 7

Being honest feels better than holding your true feelings inside.

Hiding how you really feel can lead to resentment that grows over time.

Being honest may be uncomfortable sometimes, but it's worth it to feel your best around others.

December 8

Negativity can only affect you if you are on the same frequency.

Vibrate higher!

December 9

Before you ask another to love you, make sure to love yourself first.

As you grow to love yourself more, you will begin to attract others into your life who will love you even more than you do.

December 10

Your time is precious, so don't waste it trying to please others.

Respect your boundaries and just say **no** to anything you don't want to do.

Put yourself first today.

December 11

Have the courage to say no to situations that don't please you.

By saying no to others, you are saying **yes** to yourself,

December 12

Don't wait for things to get better to feel good.

Life will always have its challenges. Feel good right here, right **now**.

There is so much joy to be had. Look around and notice the wonderful things in your life that you are not giving your attention to and focus your attention over there.

Trust the flow of life.

Everything is working out for you!

December 13

Self-doubt can hold you back from not only achieving all that you want but from even trying. Think about something you want and take a chance.

You are capable of so much more than you realize and have many unique talents. It's time to share your gifts with the world.

December 14

Spend your time around people who make you feel good, and don't waste your time on anyone else. They are not worth your energy.

If this means canceling plans or saying no to something you don't really want to do, try to do this guilt-free.

December 15

There are no limits to what you can be, do or have. You just need to be **clear** on what it is you want. Do you have that clarity?

What is it you really want?

December 16

Your life today was created by your thoughts in the past.

Are the thoughts you are thinking now creating the future you want?

Be sure to focus forward on what you want to get there.

December 17

The answers you need don't come when your mind is busy. They are found when you silence your mind.

Take 15 minutes to sit in meditation today, be still.

December 18

Count your blessings today.

The more you focus on all the wonderful things in your life, the faster the unwanted will fade away.

December 19

Have you ever noticed that some people you feel relaxed and comfortable around and other people you feel uneasy with, but you can't see an apparent reason why?

There is always an energetic reason for this. Your feelings are guiding you towards who should be in your life and who to let go of.

Always trust the way you feel.

December 20

When you worry, you are thinking about the future.

An easy way to stop worrying is to be more in the now.

What is happening now that excites you?

December 21

Offer no resistance to life and allow things to unfold without judgment.

Be easy on yourself and **let go** of the things you can't change.

December 22

Turn the voice in your head off today, even if only for a moment.

You are not this voice, be still and know this.

December 23

Take care of your thoughts when you are alone. Be kind to yourself.

Take care of your words when you are around others. Be kind to others.

Being kind costs nothing but will help keep you happy and centered in good times and bad.

December 24

As you interact with others in your life, you may notice a feeling of comfort around some and a feeling of unease around others.

Listen to this feeling and let go of any relationships that no longer serve you.

December 25

Today will be a great day full of laughter and random surprises.

Enjoy your day!

December 26

Any time you feel good, you allow abundance, well-being, happiness, health, and great relationships to flow.

December 27

Anything you want is yours, anything!

All you need to do is **imagine** and **believe**. There are no limits to what you can do, and once you realize this, your life will move forward so fast that you will wonder why you didn't believe sooner.

December 28

You have access to non-physical energy, which is here to help you when you ask. It doesn't matter what name you give to this energy or how you connect.

What is important is that you ask for help and guidance, especially in situations where you feel stuck. You can tune into this energy anytime you need by intending to do so.

December 29

Give yourself time and space today for meditation, connect to your source, and every part of you will improve.

As you meditate, you raise your vibration, and then, the universe will line you with people and situations that match your new, improved vibration.

December 30

A new beginning is coming, and new possibilities are arising.

Take some time to plan your next adventure.

December 31

If someone has broken your trust,
don't let that stop you from trusting again.

If someone has broken your heart,
don't let that stop you from loving again.

If someone has broken your spirit,
let your spirit shine bright again!

FEED YOUR SPIRIT

FEED YOUR SPIRIT RESOURCES

Tappermation
Are you looking to transform the way you think? Unlock the power of your mind with our 15-minute EFT Tapping Meditations! Experience the fastest way to remove and replace negative thoughts by combining the power of body tapping, Brainwave entrainment, and positive affirmations. Tap into your true potential with Tappermation.

Chakra Meditation
Are you looking to connect to your inner spiritual energy and unlock a sense of peace and balance? Our 15-minute chakra music meditations are designed to help you open and activate each of your seven chakras, allowing you to align yourself with your spiritual energy and reach a state of peace and harmony.

Guided Meditations
Are you looking to relax and recharge? Our 15-minute Guided Meditations are the perfect solution for you! These powerful meditations are designed to help you reduce stress and anxiety. They include positive affirmations to replace negative thinking with positive thoughts. Experience a sense of calm and clarity while entering a deep state of relaxation.

Visit **feedyourspirit.com** to learn about all programs, products, services, and free resources.

Visit **feedyourspirit.com/meditation** for a free 15-minute meditation.

Join Feed Your Spirit for unlimited access to all meditation programs available at **feedyourspirit.com/join**.

FEED YOUR SPIRIT

ABOUT THE AUTHOR

Katherine Schneider is the founder of Feed Your Spirit and is passionate about helping others find balance and inner harmony. Katherine encourages others to tap into their highest potential and manifest their dreams through her writings and meditation programs.

Explore more at **feedyourspirit.com**

Made in the USA
Middletown, DE
31 July 2023

36040127R00110